I don't eat animals
'cos I love them you
see.

1970
Melanie Safka

The information and opinions
expressed here are my own.
If you're not sure about your
health or have any medical
concerns, go see your doctor
who may well think that this
is a load of rubbish. Of course
I agree with everything in this
book & love living my life
eating food like this & feeling
fantastic. Love Emily.

THE VEGAN BUILD^C

CHRISTMAS

CONTENTS

Foreword

Firstly I have to hold my hands up & say I'm not a 24/7 vegan...
However I do in Chris's words 'believe in what I eat' but probably
like some of you, have come up with various excuses like 'I'm too
busy', 'not ready' or simply not quite bold enough to become wholly
vegan.

Josie & I have been dabbling with a plant based lifestyle for some
time & I do see a future where the whole da Bank clan go that
way... In the meantime we love reading 'The Vegan Build' books
& experimenting with what is definitely a healthier, more ethical &
interesting diet.

Throw in the fact that this is Christmas themed & I'm fully on-board,
as not only do me & the da Bank juniors adore Christmas, but we
also often over indulge & looking within these pages I can see loads
of great ideas to help us get stuck into in a healthier festive time.

Enjoy!

Rob da Bank
Bestival founder / Family man

CHRISTO BRENNAN

Founder & Director of Custom

custom^c was originally started by just two of us in 2006 tiling bathrooms & doing general DIY. We are now a team of up to 15 builders & designers renovating ski chalets in the Alps & homes throughout the south east of England.

In 2015 I decided to turn the company vegan, from the food we eat together to the products we use in renovations. It has been such an amazing move for us, with unbelievable benefits ethically, physically, mentally, spiritually & in so many other ways. We really love Christmas time as it always coincides with the completion of our mountain projects. By the end of December we are all so exhausted & missing our families so much, that we start fantasising about loading the vans, hitting play on the Chris Rea classic & setting off on the 800 mile journey home to the Isle of Wight. My girlfriend Emily, also one of our designers, painters & colour specialists, decided to put together all our favourite Christmas recipes here in 'The Vegan Build Christmas' to show how totally fulfilling a Vegan Christmas can be… delicious roasts, amazing puddings & divine cocktails.

Indulge this Christmas with a clear conscience.

ETHICS

Believe in what you eat.

REASONS TO BE VEGAN

Animals- I don't think that I am more important than any other species. I don't want something to suffer because I like to taste it.

Cost- I like a budget. I hate waste & if something can be done cheaply without excess, I feel like it should. Turkeys & cheese cost a fortune.

Health- I want to be healthy & feel good. I want to get up on Boxing Day ready for round two, with maybe even a bike ride before we start.

Planet- Take care of where we live. It's not ours to fuck up because we want to have more than the planet has to go round.

Spirituality- Pick any religion or spiritual belief & you'll pretty much always find that not killing & not stealing are high up on the list of important things to follow. No animal would ever willingly give up their life or the milk for their baby.

Vanity- I am vain! I don't want a big swollen stomach, blotchy skin or cellulite for New Years Eve, or any other time of year.

Femininity- I am a girl & I don't want to use other females' reproductive systems as a commodity that can be bought or sold.

Masculinity- I am a guy & I don't want to have excess oestrogen in my system.

WHAT'S IN SEASON IN DECEMBER...

Almonds	Chestnuts
Beetroot	Hazelnuts
Brazil nuts	Kale
Brussels sprouts	Leeks
Butternut squash	Onions
Cabbage	Parsnips
Cauliflower	Potatoes (main crop)
Celery	Swede

NOT IN SEASON

The oldest known captive turkey was 12 years old. Their gobble gobble can be heard for up to a mile & they each have their own distinctive voice. Turkeys have amazing memories, they make friends with each other for life & learn the details of an area over 1,000 acres in size. The long fleshy skin over a male's beak is called a snood, when he's excited, his head turns blue & when he's up for a fight, it turns red. They also puff up their feathers to attract the ladies. Wild turkeys can fly up to 55 mph for a short time. Baby turkeys (poults) can't fly for the first couple of weeks of life, so their mama stays with them on the ground to keep them safe until they are strong enough to get up into the trees. Turkeys were sacred in ancient Mayan and Aztec religions. The turkey was deified as Chalchiuhtotolin, the "jewelled bird".

ORGANIC

Real food

If organic fruit & veg is available in the supermarket, buy it. It costs us about ten quid more per shop & most people would spend that on a bottle of wine or crap bit of cake & coffee from a global coffee chain. Don't be tight with yourself or the planet, you're not saving, you're losing out. Put good things into your body, be gentle to the earth, soil, rivers & all the other animals. It tastes better too!

'I SAY A LITTLE PRAYER'

Burt Bacharach 1966

Gratitude is valued by all religions & spiritual beliefs. Throughout all cultures & across all languages.

'I BLESS THIS FOOD & LET IT NOURISH ME.'

Say thanks to whomever cooked it, bought it, the field that grew it, the sun that shone on it & the world for always providing enough for you.

Blessing food is an amazing thing to do & it changes the molecular structure too!

(Take a look at Masaru Emoto's amazing work.)

HOMEMADE

Crap but wholesome.

Keep waste to a minimum. Make some home made decorations or get the kids to make them. Wrap presents in newspaper or old wallpaper. Make your own crackers from toilet rolls with things in you will actually keep & use. Get presents that are organic or fair trade or from the car boot!

'GIVE A LITTLE BIT'

Roger Hodgson 1977

Donate some cash to a charity.
Whichever is closest to your heart. It feels
amazing when you do & it makes the
world a better, kinder, more caring place
to be. Give to animal rights charities or
ones supporting people with mental health
issues, donate to environmental causes or
children who don't have even a fraction of
the material wealth or security our kids do.
In fact - just set up a direct debit & do it all
year round.
Think of a time when you have been low
or down & someone has been kind to
you, think how grateful you felt & then
suddenly giving becomes the easiest thing
in the world to do.

GET IT ON

& keep it ethical.

Design your own Christmas t-shirt through the amazing Teemill by Rapanui. Organic & fair trade, you can follow your item right back to the start of its journey as cotton, growing in the fields of Northern India. Grown with rain water, co planting & cow poo. This is how we like to wear Christmas!

teemill.com

PREPARE

Are you exceedingly efficient, or totally laid back & don't want to have to do much on Christmas Day? Both work & we'll tell you what, why, how, when...

All of the recipes are for 6 people (unless stated) so halve, double or just crack on.

On the next few pages you'll find the order to cook things, what to keep in your cupboards & shopping lists of what you'll need on Christmas Day.

WHAT TO DO WHEN

Organised People

Freeze up to a month before

The nut roast
Gravy
Spinach sauce
Freeze the pineapple
Christmas cake

Make the day before

Marzipan cookies
Chocco mousse
Irish cream
Boil the potatoes to roast

Christmas Day

Squash puree
Parsnips & carrots
Potatoes
Yorkshire pudding
Broccoli & peas
Sprouts & kale
Cocktails
Mulled wine

The Laid Back

Make sure you have bought some great vegan snacks & vegan gravy etc.. Do the rest on Christmas Day.

Marzipan cookies
The nut roast
Parsnips & carrots
Potatoes
Broccoli & peas
Sprouts & kale
Cocktails

LARDER LOVE

What we love & why we use it...

Marigold organic vegetable bouillon powder (vegan) - It makes everything taste totally delicious.

Oil - A hot topic, coconut has a high smoke point but loads of air miles & is often not vegan due to monkeys being used to pick the coconuts. Rapeseed has a high smoke point, is from the UK but is high in erucic acid. Olive oil & sunflower oil are good but only if not heating.

Sweetener - Xylotol hardly raises the blood sugar at all but does contain an alcohol, agave is also good but does have some natural sugars & is processed. Stevia is the healthiest but some people find it has a bit of an odd taste. Any of these are better than sugar though, which disrupts your immune system, effects your hormones & mood, kills collagen (ages you) & is really inflammatory for your system.

Buckwheat flour - Because we go grain free if we can & buckwheat is a really nutritious seed. Grains are a stress for the body & cause inflammation.

Chicory coffee - Because it's caffeine free. Caffeine depletes the body of so many minerals & vitamins.

Alkaline - If it's easy to swap acid for alkaline food ,do it. E.g. Pistachios for almonds (See our first book 'THE VEGAN BUILD')

Pink salt - Full of minerals not just stripped back sodium chloride.

TVP - Textured vegetable protein, made from soya & comes in dried form. It is made from soya so not great to eat all the time. But great for easy homemade sausages.

KEEP ME HERE

Vegetables
Beetroot
Broccoli
Brussels sprouts
Carrots
Cauliflower
Celery
Garlic
Ginger
Kale
Leeks
Onions
Parsnips
Potatoes (or sweet)
Spinach
Squash (or pumpkin)

Cans & Jars
Almond butter
Coconut milk (can)
Haricot beans (can)
Mustard (whole grain)
Oil (coconut, rapeseed or avocado)
Plant milk (if not making your own)

Nuts & Seeds
Almonds -ground
              -whole
Brazil nuts
Flax seed (or linseed)
Hazel nuts
Nuts in shells
Pumpkin seeds
Sunflower seeds
Walnuts

Dry
Baking powder
Buckwheat flour
Cocoa powder
Cranberries (dried)
Desiccated coconut
Dried mixed fruit
Gluten free self raising flour
Oats
Pumpkin seeds
Raisins
Salt (pink or grey)
Smoked paprika
Stock powder
Teas (Dandelion, mint etc)
TVP (textured vegetable protein)
Xylitol/agave/stevia

Herbs & Spices
Almond extract
Black pepper
Cinnamon -sticks
                  -powder
Cloves (whole)
Cumin
Dill (dried)
Mint (fresh)
Mixed herbs (dried)
Mixed spice
Nutmeg (ground)
Parsley (fresh)
Rosemary (dried+fresh)
Sage (dried)
Smoked paprika
Thyme (dried)
Turmeric (dried)
Vanilla extract

Drinks
Fizzy water
Gin
Ginger ale
Red wine
Rum
Vodka
Whisky

Fruit
Apple
Avocados
Lemons
Limes
Oranges
Pineapples
Pink grapefruit
Satsumas

Chilled & Frozen
Firm tofu
Vegan yogurt
Peas (frozen)

Extras -
Health food shop & online
Chicory coffee
Orgran easy egg
Ombars
Lacuma powder
Lettices cheese
Rapanui T-shirts
Thompson & Scott champagne.
Wine - The Goodness Project

TAKE ME WITH YOU

Vegetables
Beetroot
Broccoli
Brussels sprouts
Carrots
Cauliflower
Celery
Garlic
Ginger
Kale
Leeks
Onions
Parsnips
Potatoes (or sweet)
Spinach
Squash (or pumpkin)

Cans & Jars
Almond butter
Coconut milk (can)
Haricot beans (can)
Mustard (whole grain)
Oil (coconut, rapeseed or avocado)
Plant milk (if not making your own)

Nuts & Seeds
Almonds -ground
         -whole
Brazil nuts
Flax seed (or linseed)
Hazel nuts
Nuts in shells
Pumpkin seeds
Sunflower seeds
Walnuts

Dry
Baking powder
Buckwheat flour
Cocoa powder
Cranberries (dried)
Desiccated coconut
Dried mixed fruit
Gluten free self raising flour
Oats
Pumpkin seeds
Raisins
Salt (pink or grey)
Smoked paprika
Stock powder
Teas (Dandelion, mint etc)
TVP (textured vegetable protein)
Xylitol/agave/stevia

Herbs & Spices
Almond extract
Black pepper
Cinnamon -sticks
          -powder
Cloves (whole)
Cumin
Dill (dried)
Mint (fresh)
Mixed herbs (dried)
Mixed spice
Nutmeg (ground)
Parsley (fresh)
Rosemary (dried+fresh)
Sage (dried)
Smoked paprika
Thyme (dried)
Turmeric (dried)
Vanilla extract

Drinks
Fizzy water
Gin
Ginger ale
Red wine
Rum
Vodka
Whisky

Fruit
Apple
Avocados
Lemons
Limes
Oranges
Pineapples
Pink grapefruit
Satsumas

Chilled & Frozen
Firm tofu
Vegan yogurt
Peas (frozen)

Extras -
Health food shop & online
Chicory coffee
Orgran easy egg
Ombars
Lacuma powder
Lettices cheese
Rapanui T-shirts
Thompson & Scott champagne.
Wine - The Goodness Project

TAKE ME

DRINK

Keep succulent...

WATER

Keep hydrated in the Christmas food & drink marathon. It will help alleviate some of the strain on your liver from all the excess food & alcohol. Try and Get 2-3 litres of water or herbal tea in throughout the day & avoid the food hangover! Think of it as a Christmas present for your liver!

GOLD JUICE

A Christmas morning kick up the arse.
Carrot, ginger & turmeric.

2 carrots

1 apple

5 cm of peeled ginger

1 tsp dried turmeric

1/2 a peeled lemon

optional - a pinch of
black pepper

A few ice cubes

Juice the carrots, apple, ginger & lemon.
Mix in the turmeric & black pepper.

(If you only have a blender add 100ml
water & 100ml apple juice instead of the
apple & just blitz the whole lot)

serves 2 large, 6 small.

HERBAL TEA

Get organic, fair trade & loose leaf if you can.
Here are some of our faves...

Dandelion - Cleanse your liver.

Cinnamon - Balance your blood sugar.

Mint - Cleanse the pallet.

Fennel - Soothe the digestive system.

Chamomile - Calm & relax.

FAKE IT PLANT MILK

For your chicory coffee, raw cereal & amazing life.

100g of either almonds, brazil or hazel nuts

1 litre of water

1 pinch of salt

1 tsp oil

Whizz up all the ingredients for 1 minute.

Leave for 5 minutes.

Whizz again for 1 minute.

If you like it more like skimmed milk add extra water.

Strain through a sieve.

If you want it really smooth pour it through some chopped-off tights.

Stores for 2-3 days in a jar in the fridge.

Use the left over mush for cakes or add to your cereal.

CHICORY COFFEE

Aromatic & alkaline.

Get it in your local health food shop. It is naturally caffeine free, cleans your liver, kidneys & is great for the digestion. Another great plus is that it doesn't remove any vitamins or minerals from your system like caffeine does. Serve black or with plant milk.

BREAK-FAST

Scrap the usual fast till lunch, its Christmas time.

Get the firm tofu out. Slice & fry for 5 mins each side. Add a few tbsp of soy sauce & cook for 1 more min. Serve up with everything else.

AVO' CHOCCO SMOOTHIE

Thick smooth chocolate.

1 ripe avocado

1 big handful baby spinach

2 tbsp cocoa powder

2 tbsp xylitol/agave/stevia

300 ml water or plant milk

A pinch of salt

Whizz up all the ingredients for 1 min.

Serves 2.

ROAR CHOCOLATE PORRIDGE!

Keep it raw, with cinnamon to balance your blood sugar.

400g oats (or buckwheat flakes if you're hardcore alkaline)

50g flax seeds

50g pumpkin seeds

4-6 tsp cocoa powder

1 tsp cinnamon

3 tbsp xylitol/stevia or drizzle agave on when served

Mix all the ingredients together.

(If you have fussy kids, grind the seeds up first so they don't notice)

Serve with almond/oat/soy milk.

Makes 6 large portions or save the rest in a jar.

SCRAMBLE IT

Orgran Vegan easy egg w/ black pepper & dill.

150g Orgran Vegan easy egg	Put the dry mix, dill & black pepper into a bowl.
720 ml water	Add the oil & water & whisk.
3 tbs oil	Cook in a frying pan for a few minutes stirring only once or twice.
2-3 tsp dried dill	
Freshly ground black pepper	Serves 6

orgran.com

NO PIGS, NO BLANKETS

12 seriously rustic, homemade sausages.

1 onion	Put the TVP, stock, herbs & boiling water in a bowl. Stir & leave for 5 mins.
2 cloves of garlic	
150g TVP	Finely chop & fry the onion & garlic in 1 tbsp oil for 5 mins.
450ml boiled water	
150g buckwheat flour	Mix everything except the rest of the oil together.
50g ground flax	
3 tsp stock powder	Make into 12 sausages (about 50g each) rolling the mixture in your hands.
2 tsp mixed herbs	
2 tbsp rapeseed oil	Fry on medium heat in 1 tbsp of oil for 10 minutes. Turning them so they brown on all sides.
1/2 tsp black pepper	

THE MAIN EVENT

Let's do this...

THE ROAST

Nutting more delicious.

In the following recipe we've made a cauliflower, hazelnut & sage roast, but mix it up! Swap the cauliflower for leeks or carrots & the hazelnuts for walnuts or sunflower seeds. Have a mess about with the herbs too... Even go Italian style with the oregano & basil.

CAULIFLOWER & HAZELNUT ROAST

1 large cauliflower	Grate or whizz up the cauliflower.
3 onions	Chop & fry the onions in 2 tbsp of oil on a medium heat for 5 mins, stirring.
3 cloves of garlic	Whizz the nuts & flax for 1 min in the food processor.
200g hazelnuts	
50g flax seeds	Add the cauliflower, garlic, stock powder, black pepper & sage to the nut mix & whizz for 5 seconds.
4 tsp stock powder	
4 tsp dried sage (or just a handful of fresh)	Add the beans, buckwheat flour, 1/2 the oil & water & whizz for another 5 seconds.
1 can of haricot beans	Add the cooked onions & mix with spoon to keep chunky.
100g buckwheat flour	
3 tbsp rapeseed oil	Oil a bread tin, or baking tray & dollop it all in.
½ tsp black pepper	
100ml water	Bake for 40 mins at 200°C

HERBY GRAVY

It's all about the onions.

2 onions	Chop & fry the onions & celery in the oil on a really low heat for 15 mins, take the lid off & cook them for another 15, both times stir them a bit.
2 cloves of garlic	
1 stick of celery	
2 tbsp oil	Add the buckwheat flour & mix & cook for 1 min.
1 tbsp mustard	
4 tbsp buckwheat flour	Turn up the heat, add the stock powder & a glug of the water (or wine), mix really well & bring to the boil.
4 tsp stock powder	
1 litre of boiling water	Add the rest of the water, turn down the heat & simmer for 10 minutes.
A handful of fresh parsley or thyme	Whizz in the blender for 30 secs.

SPINACH & NUTMEG SAUCE

Rich & smooth.

200g bag of spinach

2 cloves crushed garlic

100g oats

2 tbsp oil

3 tsp stock powder

1/2 tsp ground nutmeg

1L water

Whizz the oats & water for 1 min & then strain. (Use the oats for a face mask!)

Heat the oil on medium heat.

Add the garlic & stir for 1 min.

Add all the spinach, nutmeg & stock powder & cook for 2 mins.

Put the cooked spinach in a blender, add the oat milk & whizz for 1 min.

Return the mix to the pan & heat up to thicken for about 5 mins.

YORKSHIRE PUDS

Different but batter.

350g gluten free self-raising flour	Heat oven to 220°C
1 tsp baking powder	Whizz the water & flax for 1 min.
20g ground flaxseed	Add the flour, baking powder & salt, whizz for another min.
600ml water	Leave in the fridge for at least half an hour.
6 tsp vegetable oil	Put 1/2 tsp of oil into 12 holes of a muffin tin & put in the oven for 5 mins.
Pinch of salt	Get the boiling hot tin from the oven & pour the batter into the oil.
Muffin tin tray	Put in the oven & bake for 25-30 mins until risen.

Gluten & egg free makes these little guys a little
strange looking, but still super delicious.

PARSNIPS & CARROTS

Always roasted, with a hint of cumin.

3 big carrots

3 big parsnips

2 onions

1 tsp cumin

2 tbsp oil

1/2 tsp salt

1/2 tsp black pepper

Chop the parsnips & carrots into chunks, cutting out the core of the parsnips.

Peel & 1/4 the onions.

Put all ingredients on a baking tray & mix well.

Shove in the oven at 250°C for 50 mins, stirring once half way through.

Serves 6

POTATOES
W/ ROSEMARY

Or sweet potatoes if you're wanting to be more
alkaline or just plain fancy.

1 1/2 biggish potatoes each (you can never have too many)	Chop each potato into 4.
	Boil with salt for 10 mins.
2 tsp dried rosemary	Drain.
3 tbsp oil	Put them back in the saucepan with the oil & rosemary, put the lid on & shake them about really hard for a bit.
1 tsp salt	
	Put them all on a baking tray & into the oven at 250°C for 40 mins. Turning once half way through.

BUTTERNUT SQUASH PUREE

Smooth, comforting & smokey.

1 large squash	Halve & de-seed the squash, rub the cut side with 1 tbsp oil.
2 onions	
4 cloves garlic	Put in oven at 250°C, roast for 1 hour.
2 tbsp oil	Take out & scrape all the flesh into blender.
2 tsp stock powder	Add all other ingredients & whizz for 1 min.
2 tsp smoked paprika	

BROCCOLI & PEAS

Steam the green & keep al dente.

50g broccoli per person

80g peas per person

Chop up the broccoli & steam for 5 mins.

Add the peas & steam for another 5 mins.

80g Peas = 7g Protein

50g Broccoli = 88% RDA Vitamin K

SPROUTS & KALE

Get the wok out.

40g per person of kale (cut the stalks out if not pre-prepared)

4-5 brussels sprouts per person

2 cloves of crushed garlic

1 tbsp oil

200ml water

1/2 tsp salt

Black pepper to taste

Cut the sprouts in half.

Get the wok or frying pan really hot, add the oil & the sprouts.

Cook for 2 mins, stir & cook for another 2 mins.

Add the garlic & 100 ml water, put a lid on & cook for 2 mins.

Add the salt, pepper, kale, 100ml water, stir well, put the lid on & cook for 2 more mins.

Serve immediately.

5 Sprouts = 185% RDA Vitamin K
40g Kale = 109% RDA Vit A + 408% RDA Vitamin K

WIGHT SOUP

Boxing Day soup - simple & comforting.

1 tbsp oil	Chop & fry the onions for 5 mins.
2 onions	Chop the rest of the veg up quite small & whack it in with the garlic too.
2 cloves crushed garlic	Add the stock & water & boil for 5 mins untill everything cooked.
2 leeks	Add the herbs & then whizz for 1 min.
1 large cauliflower (700-800g ish)	Serve up in a bowl or mug with some toasted rye bread & watch another movie.
200g potatoes	Serves 6
4 tsp stock powder	
1L boiling water	'Thorfinn bowl'
2 tsp dried dill or parsley (or a handful of fresh)	by Elli at 'Isle of Celandine' www.isleofcelandine.com

DESSERT

Pudding, afters, nibbles & treats.

CHRISTMAS CAKE

Refined sugar free, raw & totally divine.

250g raisins

200g chopped pecans or walnuts

200g mixed peel

150g ground almonds

50g desiccated coconut
(& extra to sprinkle on the top)

50g ground flax

50g sunflower seeds

2 large oranges (both juice & zest)

1 tsp vanilla extract

1 tsp mixed spice

1 tsp cinnamon

2 cm chunk peeled fresh ginger

1 tbsp oil

3 tbsp water or booze

A pinch of salt

In a blender, add the orange juice, ginger, 3 tbsp of water or booze & half the raisins. Whizz for 2 mins.

Add the rest of the raisins, all the spices, vanilla, orange zest & salt. Whizz for 1 more min.

In a clean blender jug, add the coconut & seeds & whizz for 10 secs (we want it a bit lumpy). Add the peel & nuts & whizz for 2 more secs.

Put the two mixes together, give it a good mix.

Press into a lined & oiled cake tin, 15cm across. Leave in the fridge overnight.

Take out of the tin, sprinkle with some coconut & decorate, slice up & serve.

CHOCCO ORANGE

Intense...

3 cans coconut milk

2 tbsp xylitol/agave/stevia

3 tbsp cocoa powder

Zest of 2 unwaxed oranges

Open the cans of coconut & scoop the cream off the top & put in the whizzer.

Whizz everything together but leave a bit of orange zest to decorate. (If too thick to whizz add a splash of water)

Dollop into 6 little jars/bowls/tins.

Chill in the fridge until you're ready to eat them.

If it's warm in your house, put the un opened cans of milk in the fridge for an hour to make sure the milk seperates. You're after just the really thick cream from the top.

PINEAPPLE & MINT SORBET

Cleanse...

1 large ripe pineapple

20 mint leaves

Juice of 2 limes

Slice all of the skin off & cut out the core of the pineapple.

Chop into chunks & put into a bag & freeze. (Freeze up to a month beforehand)

Take out of the freezer 30 mins before serving.

Put all of the chunks & lime juice into a food processor and whizz (or use a hand blender).

Chop the fresh mint & add to the mix & whizz for 3 seconds.

Serves 4-6.

MARZIPAN COOKIES

Makes 12 delicious melt-in-the-mouth cookies.

250g ground almonds	Put the oven onto 180°C
50g coconut oil	Melt the oil in a saucepan.
100g xylitol/agave/stevia	Add everything else except the water & mix well.
30g ground flax	(If the mix isn't sticking together in a ball add a splash of water.)
1 tsp baking powder	Divide into 12, roll into balls & flatten slightly.
1 tsp almond extract	Put onto a tray covered with greaseproof paper.
A pinch of salt	Bake in the oven for 9-10 mins. (They don't look done but firm up when cool).
A pinch of turmeric	
Juice of 1/2 a lemon	
A splash of water to bring it together	

SANTA'S BALLS

Cranberry, beetroot & almond balls.

75g raw peeled beetroot

200g ground almonds

30g ground flax

75g dried cranberries
(usually sweetened, if not
add some xylitol or agave)

100ml water

1/2 tsp vanilla extract

Peel & chop the beetroot into small chunks.

Turn round & pretend to everyone you've cut your finger off with the beetroot juice all over your hands.

Whizz the beetroot & water.

Add the cranberries to the beetroot & whizz for 1 min.

Put all the ingredients into a bowl & mix.

Roll into 25 small balls. Sprinkle with extra ground almonds.

These will keep for 3 days in the fridge.

LACUMA FUDGE

Heavenly!

170g unsalted almond butter

100g coconut oil

30g xylitol/stevia

50g lacuma powder or cocoa

1/2 tsp vanilla extract

A tiny pinch of salt

If you can't get the lacuma (Peruvian toffee flavour fruit) don't worry, just make chocolate fudge instead using cocoa powder.

Whizz the xylitol or stevia into a powder like icing sugar.

Put everything in a saucepan on really low heat & stir until all melted.

Place in a small tub or into a rubber ice cube tray.

Put in the fridge for a couple of hours

Cut up or pop out.

These will keep for 3 days in the fridge.

CHOCOLATE HEAVEN

Ombar tick all the boxes; ethical, raw, vegan, organic & refined-sugar free! This is the most amazing chocolate we have ever tasted, vegan or not. There are so many good flavours to try, including Coco Mylk, 72% Cocoa & Mandarin, seriously delicious!

ombar.co.uk

I'M NUT ASKING

I'm telling you.

The most wonderfully healthy thing about Christmas is that suddenly the supermarket aisles are rammed with bags & bags of nuts to crack. Raw & full of fibre, vitamins & minerals. Steer clear of the peanuts & get stuck in!

ALMONDS - Skin hair & nails (Vitamin E)

BRAZILS - Testicle power (Selenium)

HAZELNUTS - Muscles, nerves, bones (Magnesium)

PECANS - Metabolism, nervous system (Vitamin B1)

WALNUTS - Brain & joint function (Omega 3)

SATSUMAS!

Don't underestimate these little orange vitamin balls.
A good satsuma is a heavenly thing. Super juicy & full of
flavour, one satsuma delivers 36g of Vitamin C
(that's 60% of your RDA for the day!)

VITAMIN C is AMAZING! An essential nutrient for the
body, it is needed for the development & maintenance of
blood vessels, repairing scar tissue & cartilage. It's hugely
anti-inflammatory, anti-aging & helps with collagen
synthesis. It's a powerful antioxidant & protects your body
from free radicals & everyday environmental damage
including UV. It is needed for normal immune function
& aids the proper absorption of iron. It also is a natural
antihistamine. The body cannot store this vitamin so it is
needed daily. Cooking kills Vitamin C by up to 75% so
keep things as raw as you can (harder at Christmas but
easy in the summer). Keep your intake of vitamin C high
& feel fabulous all season!

VEGAN CHEESES

Lovingly creating artisan small batch cheese. Lettices is on a mission to make ethical & healthy food affordable, tasty & an easy choice.

Camembear, Blue Beauty, Smokey Bakon spread & lots more… Get yourself some buckwheat crackers, onion chutney & get stuck in.

www.lettices.com

SOME-THING STRONGER

The most alkaline, low sugar, raw beverages we could make. Bottoms up.

VEGAN IRISH CREAM

Raw, alkaline & sugar free.

50g desiccated coconut

100g almonds

500ml water

150ml water

75ml whisky

50g xylitol/agave/stevia

1 tsp vanilla extract

1 tbsp chicory powder (p.48) or instant coffee if you don't mind caffeine

1 tsp cocoa powder

A pinch of salt

1/2 tsp oil

In your blender add 500ml of water, the almonds, coconut, salt & oil.

Blend for 1 min.

Wait 5 minutes, then blend again for 1 min.

Sieve the mixture through a really fine sieve, or the foot of a pair of thin tights.

Add everything else to the liquid & blend for 5 secs. Serve with ice.

Play party games…

Packed with protein, magnesium & tonnes of Vitamins E & B2

BUBBLY

Champagne & Prosecco

We love a glass of Champagne to celebrate the end of a build at Christmas time.
Thomson & Scott really know what they are doing & produce the most amazing Champagne & Prosecco. Vegan, organic, low sugar & low sulphite too, everything we want in a glass of bubbly. Their message is simple - "Cut sugar, drink better, one fabulous glass at a time."

thomsonandscott.com

PINK HOUND

As alkaline as it gets.

6 red or pink grapefruit (1.2l)

150 -300ml vodka or gin (depending on how strong you like it)

6 sprigs of rosemary

Halve the grapefruits & squeeze the juice through a sieve into a jug.

Add the alcohol & stir.

Serve with a sprig of rosemary.

(If you don't have rosemary just dip the top of the glass in the booze before you pour & dip into pink salt. You now have a salty dog!)

Serves 6

GINGER STORM

Anti-inflamatory ginger, one step ahead of the hang over!

Per Person.	Pour ginger ale into your favourite glass.
200ml ginger ale	
	Add the rum.
25ml dark rum	
	Serve with chopped lime & a slice of fresh ginger.
1 slice fresh ginger	
1/2 lime	

Make sure you buy a ginger ale that has real ginger extract & no refined sugar. Most supermarkets will stock a good one alongside some really naff rubbish-filled ones.

MULLED WINE

Made with vegan, organic, sulphite-free wine from The Goodness Project.
They have an amazing range of wines & also stock delicious
gluten-free beers too.

2 bottles of vegan red wine

1tsp of cinnamon

1 tsp of cloves

1/2 tsp ground nutmeg

6 slices of fresh ginger

1/2 tsp vanilla extract

2 tbsp xylitol or agave

Zest & juice of 2 oranges

1 orange sliced

Mix everything together except the orange juice in a saucepan with only a glug of wine.

Whisk & cook for 5 mins.

Add the rest of the wine & orange juice & add some orange slices too if you're feeling fancy.

If you want it quite alcoholic don't cook for too long or if you prefer lower alcohol bring it to the boil & simmer for 5 mins.

Serve up & sing some carols.

custom ^c

Hi I'm Emily & I work for a company called Custom who co-created & published this book with me. Custom are proud to be an ethical, interior architecture, design & build company. The team ranges from builders to colour specialists, from chippies to project managers. We all share the same core passions, being as active, healthy & vegan as is humanly possible.

We love creating amazing spaces our clients love living in & we thought we'd take the next few pages to show some of our most recent projects, in the beautiful & very Christmassy, snow covered French Alps.

Lots of love *emily*

DESIGN IT
BUILD IT
LIVE IT

The Cabin

Solaise Plein Sud

The Loft

Will & Isaac at The Cabin

The Cabin

Sainte Foy
Our French home village

The Squirrels
Custom's French HQ

A few of the Custom
Vegan Build team

Photo by Pal Hanson

ME

My name is Emily

I am a painter, decorator & colour specialist. I am the creator of this book & a passionate vegan. I am a single mumma to amazing, creative, loving, fabulous Athene Blossom & part time step mum to beautiful & aware Christabel & super-cool Bowie. I am enthusiastic, passionate & scruffy. I have always adored colour & almost everything I do is affected by it at some level. Design & construction fills my heart & head & I just love finding creative solutions that work. Authentic communication & the transition of everything is what makes me tick. I love swimming in the sea, going to car boots to find everything I could ever possibly need & having fancy-dress parties, especially when Florence Poppy Deary is there. I am also totally madly in love with Christo Brennan, the most handsome man I ever met.

emilyandcolour.com

THE JOURNEY

We are so excited to be showing the world how strong, fit, healthy & fulfilling simple vegan food can be. Everything we do is vegan, alkaline, gluten & refined sugar-free, affordable, simple & totally delicious.
This little Christmas book is the second in the series so far. Our first cook book 'The Vegan Build' was originally written for the **custom**ᶜ design & build team to show how we cook & eat every day after a hard days work.
We love Christmas time & so have made 'The Vegan Build Christmas' showing how to knock up amazing, no fuss Christmas food with all the trimmings.
Keep your eyes peeled for the next in the series - 'The Vegan Build Kids', a recipe & meal planner with detailed nutritional information & advice based on our three invincible vegan children: Athene, Bowie & Christabel.

STOCKISTS

The most ethical, vegan products for Christmas & your whole life. Most of these are also organic, low sugar & gluten free.

Rapanui ethical clothing & design your own t-shirt - Online
rapanuiclothing.com & teemill.com

Orgran Vegan Easy Egg - Health food shops, supermarkets.
orgran.com

Ombar Vegan Chocolate - Health food shops, Waitrose.
ombar.com

Lettices Vegan Cheese & Meat - Online only.
lettices.com

Thompson & Scott Champagne & Prosecco -Ocado, Amazon.
thompsonandscott.com

Wines, Beers & Spirits - The Goodness Project - Online only.
thegoodnessproject.co.uk

INDEX

Are chrismas List

eat
- 1 Vegea crismas frie
- 2 Pet roben
- 3 Nick roodog
- 4 meet the chrismas fairy
- 5 Mack chrismas ice-clim
- 6 Do some prilling
- 7 Don't eat Mins pie
- 8 or rost chicen
- 9 Mack prox & Bulgoi zawt gils chrismas
- 10 capcher jeasos becourse
- 11 remember flos birthday

THANK YOU

Athene - For being so patient & supportive through all the hours I spent working on this, for being my kid & wriggling in my bed & for snuggling me & loving guinea pigs.

Christo - For being so handsome, confident & Sagitarian. For being so ridiculously positive at all times & being as extreme as me in life.

Florence - For being my sister & all your technical help, both in life & on the computer. For being so creative, passionate, intense & outrageous.

Bo & Bel - For trying recipes & being such passionate mini vegans.

Smiler - For the perfect timing with the camera loan.

My gorgeous friends - For being such amazing women. For always listening, talking & understanding through everything that happens in our lives; Nicola, Becky, Jaime.

Martin & Katie - For being the ultimate vegan builders & for all the unwavering support from wherever you are in the world.

Shiloh - For never minding about being sat in the van or on a building site or climbing mountains in the snow.

For recipe testing - Nicola, Katie, Claire.

Will & Mike - For proof reading & not judging me for being so awful at spelling & grammar. (or at least pretending not to!)

This book was passionately written, designed, photographed, tried & tested on the Isle of Wight.